Selections from the early print-newspapers in colonial Calcutta, India (1780-1820). (Heteroglossic print, diseases and fashion)

TAPATI BHARADWAJ

Copyright © 2014 Tapati Bharadwaj

All rights reserved.

ISBN: 8192875288
ISBN-13: 978-8192875286

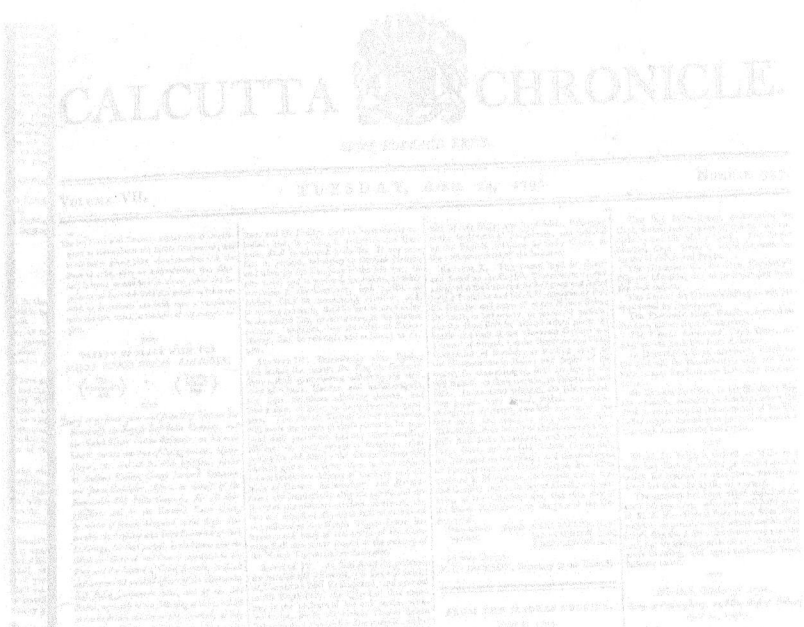

DEDICATION

To the carnivalesque-ness within indian society.

# CONTENTS

|   |   |   |
|---|---|---|
|   | Acknowledgments | i |
| 1 | Introduction | 7 |
| 2 | Multilingual texts | 11 |
| 3 | Diseases and filth | 17 |
| 4 | Fashion and habits of consumption | 21 |
| 5 | Poetry, print and the press | 37 |
| 6 | Appendix | 59 |

# CALCUTTA CHRONICLE

## ACKNOWLEDGMENTS

Everyone in the team at *Facsimile, A Center for Early Print and Society* has been tremendously kind in their involvement.

# 1 INTRODUTION

The newspapers that were printed in the early years of print culture in colonial Bengal, in the last two decades of the eighteenth century, give us vivid insights into the social and cultural lives of the settler British community. More interestingly, though, we are allowed glimpses into how Natives were seen from the perspective of the Britishers. More often than not, native practices and customs were construed as being visual phantasgormic spectacles. The following report in the *Calcutta Gazette* in 1788 describes a human sacrifice, as if a macabre, theatrical experience:

> We are credibly informed, that on the night of the Sunday the 6$^{th}$ instant, which was the night of the new moon, a human sacrifice was actually offered to *Kaly* , the Hindoo Goddess of Destruction, at her temple at Chitpore. This horrid rite was performed under cover of the dark night by persons as yet unknown; but the next morning the following circumstances were observed. The door of the Pagoda had been opened in the night, said by some to have been broken open; the trunk of the man sacrificed was found before the threshold, and the head within the Pagoda, at the feet of the Idol, which had been invested, during the sacrifice, with new robes made of rich and costly manufactures, and several new necklaces, and bracelets

of gold and silver. The utensils and vessels necessary to such a sacrifice, were also left in the Pagoda, and appeared to have been prepared with an exact conformity to the precepts of those books of the Hindoos in which such sacrifices are recommended. And in a word everything tended to raise a suspicion, that the whole was the performance of some opulent and well-read Hindoo. The poor wretch who was the victim, appeared to be of the *Chendal* Cast, which is an inferior tribe of villagers; and this, it seems, is the cast from which such sacrifices are ____ to be made.

The Foujdar has, it is said, seized the Bramin that usually attends the Pagoda, in order to discover who are the persons concerned in this murder; but nothing has yet transpired.[1]

The cultures and customs of the Indians were sometimes incomprehensible to the ruling Britishers, but they, being newly established rulers, were compelled to figure out ways to understand the Natives better.

One particular news report in 1788 described how some salt manufacturers (and once can assume that they must have been poor) were so touched by the behavior of a Britisher that they made a figure of him so that they could worship it:

> It is a fact that the conduct of Mr. H*****l, in the Sunderbunds, has been so exemplary and mild towards the poor Molungees or Salt Manufactures, that to express their gratitude they have made a representation of his figure or image, which they worship

---

[1] The Calcutta Gazette, Thursday April 24, 1788, Vol.9, No.217, p.2, column.1

amongst themselves. A strong proof that the natives of this country are sensible of kind treatment, and easily governed without coercive measures.[2]

The non Native population of rulers could live by identifying themselves as separate from the Natives; by the end of the eighteenth century, realms of institutional power were established in the colonies and in the process, imperial identity was formed intrinsic to maintaining a territory. Print culture was one such import that made colonial control possible. The realm of print was both spatial (through acts of reading) and a geo-physical domain (the realm of printers and type foundries). This was akin to many other realms that emerged in the last two decades of the eighteenth century: the emergence of multilingual printed texts in Calcutta, as it developed into a westernized city with loads of diseases, the import of western habits of consumption into the colonies and the establishment of a print induced sub-public sphere. The print induced communication circuit was one such realm which existed in conjunction with the other institutional and disciplinary realms.

This book (the second in the series) has a selection from the early newspapers that had been printed in the early years of the British-East India Company, that is between 1780-1820, in colonial Calcutta, India. How do we read these texts that were written centuries ago and make sense of the printed texts? We cannot elide the fact that they were meant to be textually consumed by the Britishers who had arrived in India as part of the package of colonization.

Reading primary texts alters how we theorize. The newspapers allow us to peek into this newly emerging world in Bengal and

---

[2] The Calcutta Gazette, Thursday April 24, 1788, Vol.9, No.217, p.2, column.1.

how socio-technological changes were taking place. We seem to think that these changes seamlessly moved into Bengal without any hiccups. We rarely do have access to these primary texts, as they are hidden in archives. What emerges is the human face of the process of British colonization and not an abstract concept of absolute power.

## THE COMMUNICATION CIRCUIT AND THE REALMS OF POWER.

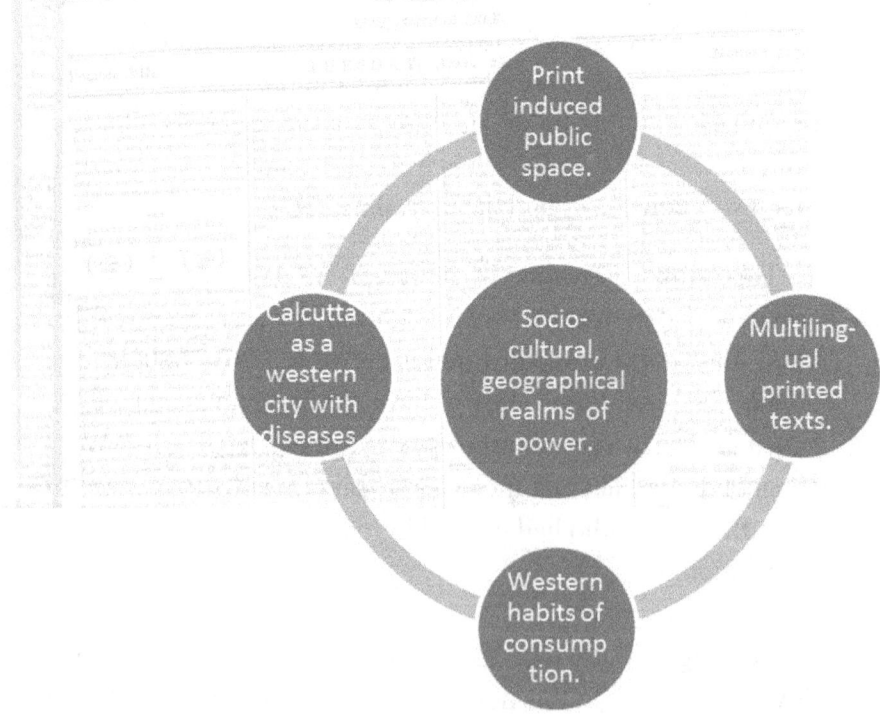

## 2 MULTILINGUAL TEXTS

There is a moment in the history of the English printed newspaper that emerged in Calcutta in the last two decades of the eighteenth century that defies all logic; when we consider the history of the newspaper and try to understand as to what was it that allowed it to transform itself whereby news was printed simultaneously in three different languages, we are unable to arrive at any coherent answer. The printed newspaper that evolved in Britain had a logic of its own (for more see Appendix A).

But, when print was transferred to India, it followed a trajectory that was particularly its own. It was introduced under colonization, undoubtedly but the manner in which print technology transmuted itself is not very clear. The heteroglossic newspaper that emerged, thus, was a pastiche of sorts – and in this particular context, more so as a single news item was printed in multiple languages simultaneously on the same page. This heteroglossic text reveals a particular moment in the initial moments of colonial presence in Calcutta, and in many ways, reflects the multilingual nature of

Indian society. To understand this phenomenon more comprehensively, Mikhail Bakhtin's notion of how heteroglossia functions in a novel is quite pertinent.[3] Bakhtin writes that at any given moment of its evolution, language is stratified" into linguistic dialects but also into "languages that are socio-ideological: languages of social groups" and therefore, "literary language [used in novels] itself is only one of these heteroglot languages."[4] Language, therefore, is a reflection of society. It is reductive to look at language outside its social matrix and for Bakhtin, at any "given historical moment of verbal-ideological life," each generation has its own language, and therefore, "at any given moment, languages of various epochs and periods of socio-ideological life cohabit with one another."[5] The heteroglot nature of language represents the "co-existence of socio-ideological contradictions between the present and the past, between differing epochs of the past, between different socio-ideological groups in the present."[6] This coexistence of different linguistic styles and

---

[3] Mikhail Bakhtin, *The Dialogic Imagination*, edited by Michael Holquist (Austin: University of Texas Press, 2004). Heteroglossia, once incorporated into the novel ... is another's speech in another's language, serving to express authorial intentions but in a refracted way. Such speech constitutes a special type of double-voiced discourse. It serves two speakers at the same time and expresses simultaneously two different intentions... And all the while these two voices are dialogically interrelated, they... know about each other... it is as if they actually hold a conversation with each other." (p. 324)

[4] Ibid., p. 272.

[5] Ibid., p. 290-291.

[6] Ibid., p. 291.

languages is an example of hybridization; which is a mixture of two social languages within the limits of a single utterance.[7]

The multilingual newspaper allowed the convergence of multiple languages that had and existed in different social moments in the history of India: English was the language of the new British rulers, while Persian had been used earlier and Bengali was the language in use by the inhabitants of Bengal. The hegemonic present of colonial rule, the native present and the immediate past all featured in this heteroglot text, creating the illusion of linguistic parity while in reality that was not the case. Examining the reasons as to why such a multilingual text would exist does give us an opportunity to understand the heterogeneous nature of Indian society.

---

[7] Ibid., p. 358.

Selections from the early newspaper print in colonial Calcutta.

**An example of a multilingual newspaper text from The <u>Calcutta Gazette</u>, 1788. (Advertisements of goods)**

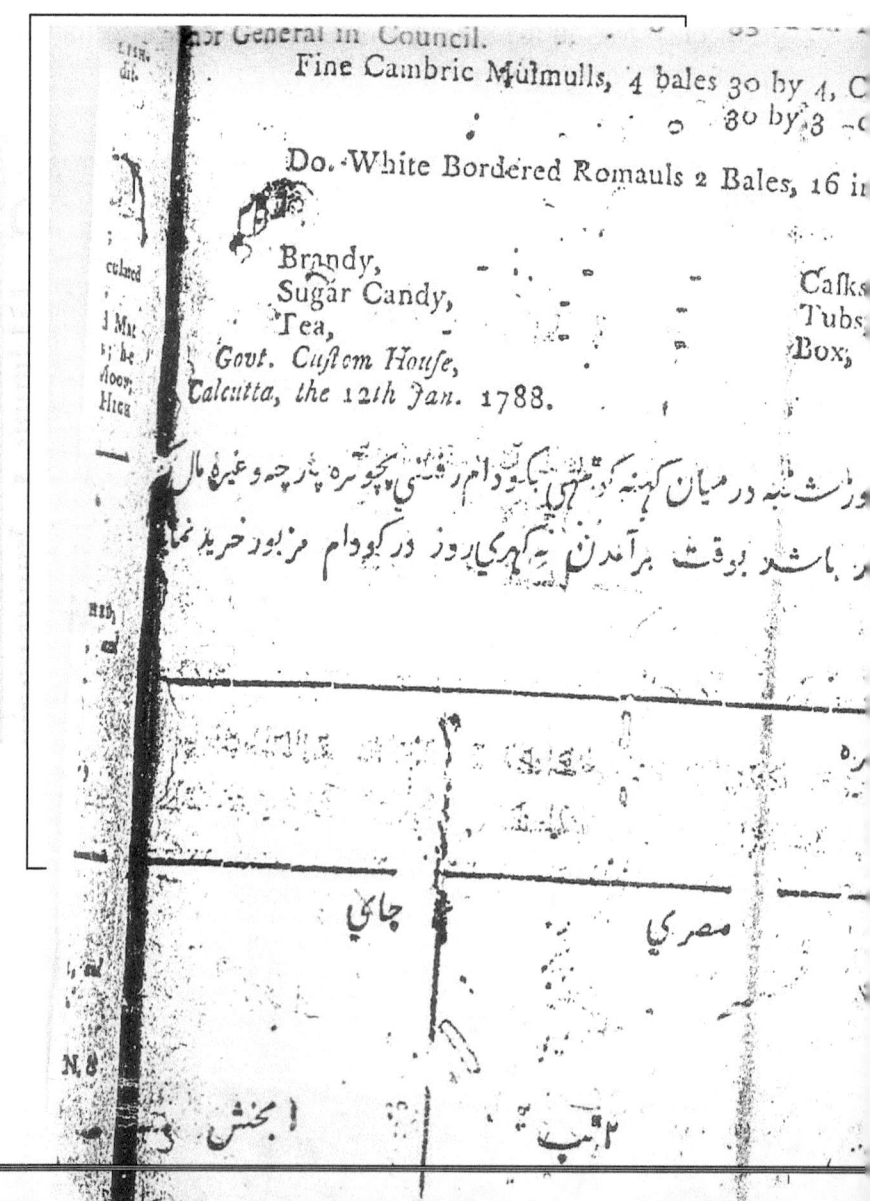

Selections from the early newspaper print in colonial Calcutta.

# An example of a multilingual newspaper text: an advertisement for the sale of Bibles.

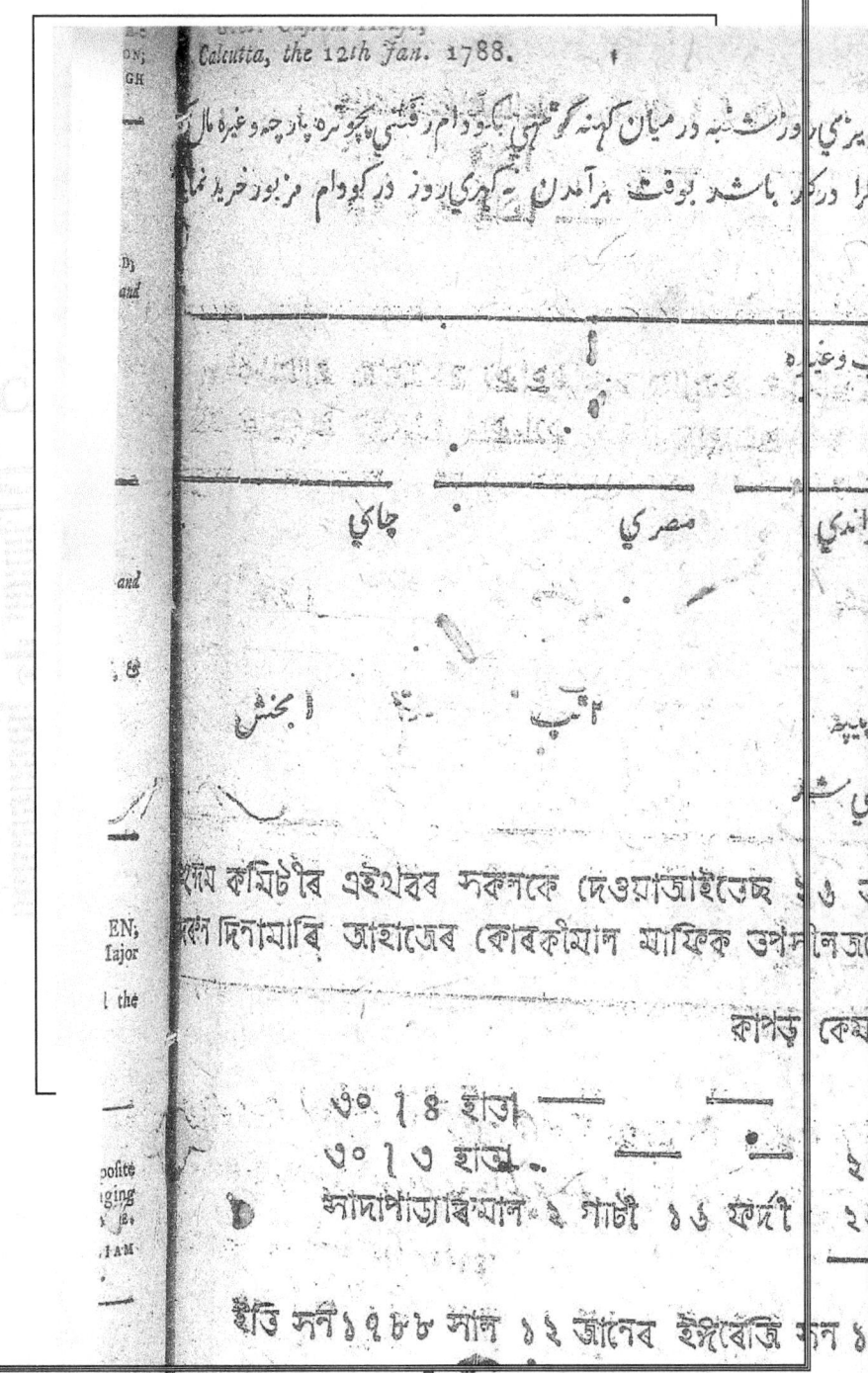

**An example of a multilingual newspaper text: an advertisement of salt being sold.**

## 3 DISEASES AND FILTH.

Did those Britishers who travelled to Calcutta towards the end of the eighteenth century arrive at a city that was extremely different from what they had left behind? In many ways, the dirt and squalor and the surrounding chaos of native life existed alongside the "white" city of Calcutta where there were beautiful, palatial houses and this was in some ways akin to what London was in the eighteenth century. By 1716, London was the largest European city and it was changing from a "compact traditional city to a rambling heterogeneous metropolis."[8] There was rapid migration, about 8,000 annually, of young people and women who were needed as servants and workers for burgeoning industries, and these migrants settled in densely packed neighbourhoods "marked by open sewers, decaying rubbish, virulent diseases and overflowing graveyards."[9] The streets were filled with the vulnerable part of the population, begging for a living and on the border of poverty. As Sophie Gee argues, that a "glut of waste matter fills the pages of eighteenth-century literature – not just in minority texts but in canonical works such as *Paradise Lost*, *The Tale of a Tub*, "A Modest Proposal," and *A Journal of the Plague Year*."[10] She

---

[8] Walking the Streets of Eighteenth- century London, John Gay's Trivia *(1716)*, eds. Clare Brant and Susan E Whyman, "Introduction," New York: OUP, 2007, p. 4.

[9] Ibid., p. 4.

[10] Sophie Gee, Making Waste, Leftovers and the Eighteenth-Century Imagination (Princeton, Princeton UP, 2009), p. 2-3. In Making Waste, the first book about

goes on to write that this waste is "nothing if not memorable: Milton's infernal dregs, Swift's odious excrements, Pope's pissing contexts, Defoe's corpses."[11] At that time, this waste was supposed to be ignored but English writers were quite explicit in how waste was described – "[d]ung, guts, and mud, dead dogs and turnip tops, sweep through the pages of eighteenth-century writing."[12] Maybe, in reality, it was not all that difficult for the Britishers to live in Calcutta, making us suspect their ramblings on how terrible life was in the colonial city.

**ON SCAVENGERS:**

From: <u>The Calcutta Gazette</u>, Thursday, May 1, 1788, Vol.9, No.218, p.3, column.3

Police

WANTED

By the Commissioners of Police,

PERSONS to execute the Office of SCAVENGER and DEPUTY SCAVENGER, for the Town of Calcutta – Application is desired to be made to Mr. HUGH HONYCOMB, Secretary to the Commissioners, on or before the 6<sup>th</sup> day of May next, from whom

---

refuse and its place in Enlightenment literature and culture, Sophie Gee examines the meaning of waste at the moment when the early modern world was turning modern. Bernard Mandeville, praising English prosperity in *The Fable of the Bees*, told Londoners to treasure the dunghills in the streets, the running drains, animals, and crowds of beggars as daily reminders of London's wealth. p.2-3.

[11] Ibid., p.3.

[12] Ibid., p. 2-3.

information may be had respecting the duties expected to be performed.

By Order of the Commissioners,

H. HONYCOMB.

Fort William, April 23, 1788.

## ON PARIAH DOGS.

As I was Jogging along in my Palanqueen yesterday, I could not avoid observing without a kind of secret concern for the health of several of my tender and delicate Friends, a String of Paria Dogs without an Ounce of Hair on some of them and in the last stage of the Meange plunge in and refresh themselves very comfortably in the great Tank – …
The great increase of Filth in it must likewise add to its impurity and contribute not a little to give it that Raw disagreeable smell which is very perceptible upon a Comparative trial with other Waters.[13]

## ON CHOLERA AND DISEASES

From The Calcutta Gazette, Thursday, June 18$^{th}$, 1818, #1790.

To THE EDITOR OF THE
**CALCUTTA GAZETTE**

---

[13] April 15$^{th}$-22$^{nd}$, 1780, pp. 2-3.

Mr. Editor

I am sorry to learn from the Calcutta papers that the Cholera Morbus still rages in Bengal. I have made Translations from Syndenham and Celsus on the subject, which, perhaps you may think worthy of a place in your paper.

Syndenham treats of it as an epidemic in England in 1669, and his authority used to be deemed excellent. I do not need to give you his description of the disease, as it quite the same as is mentioned in the Bengal papers. You will see, that his reasonings and practice do not agree with those of some of your very wise Bengal Assistant Surgeons, who are held up in Government orders as reaches to us all, and who seem to think it unnecessary to refer to books for the experience of their predecessors – being perfectly satisfied with what they call their own discoveries. The Rice is no longer new; and large doses of calomel even, though given in powder, seem to have but little confidence placed in them, however worthy of it.

I am, Mr. Editor,
Your most obedient Servant,
A MADRAS MEDICAL OFFICER.

Camp near Poonah.

## 4 FASHION AND HABITS OF CONSUMPTION

A large section of the newspapers that were printed in Calcutta were filled with advertisements, because without advertisements in newspapers, goods that were brought from Europe could not be publicly made known to the residents. The men could not do without claret and cheeses, and the women could not survive without stockings and hats. The relationship between traders, the European residents of Bengal and print culture is an intrinsic one for goods that were imported and advertised through print, and sold to the English residents. This was the function of print advertisements, and a public notice set up in 1768 in a commercial area of Calcutta, by one William Bolts, addressed to the "Public", draws -attention to the importance of print technology: "Mr Bolts takes this method of informing the public that the want of a printing press in this city being of great disadvantage in business, and making it extremely difficult to communicate such intelligence to the community as is of the utmost importance to every British subject."[14] And even if the newspaper had little circulation and subscription, advertisements made it economically possible for the newspaper to be printed.

---

[14] Quoted in Thankappan Nair, A History of the Calcutta Press (Calcutta: Firma KLM, 1987), p. 1.

Newspaper publishers were fully cognizant of this fact and took advantage of the consumer fetishism displayed by the British. All newspapers had an alternative title; the full title of the *Bengal Gazette* was the *Bengal Gazette or Calcutta General Advertiser*, likewise the *India Gazette* was also subtitled *India Gazette, or Calcutta Public Advertiser*. These social habits of consumption made it possible for the rich and the educated English to live in India. Those who lived in Calcutta had similar habits of consumption and they were bound to the metropole of London through these social habits.

## ADVERTISEMENTS.

The Calcutta Gazette or the Oriental Advertiser.
Vol. viii. Thursday, November 1, 1787, No. 192.

On Monday night was married Charles Wyatt, Esq. of the Corps of Engineers, to Mrs. Drake, widow of the late Mr. Drake of the Bombay establishment. The ceremony was performed about 8 o'clock, by the Reverend Mr. Blanchard, in the New Church.

The reigning dress of the Ladies at the balls of the Carnivals in Naples and France, are a domino of taffeta of the colour 'queue de forin," i.e. tails of a gold finch; decorated at the head, hands and fore-part, with artificial roses, and flounced around the bottom with white gauze, tied with two garlands of roses. The hair is dressed in very small curls all over, and two large ones flowing down each side of the neck. Behind is a large Chignon, falling very low; the ear-rings are plain gold a la plaquette; the shoes are rose satin, trimmed with white satin ribbons.

CALCUTTA GAZETTE
Thursday. March 12, 1818. No. 1776.

HEALTH, BEAUTY, A CLEAR COMPLEXION, AND A GOOD COMPLEXION.

## WILLIAM SMYTHE

Has the pleasure of informing the Public, that he has received by the last Ship from London,

A VERY ELEGANT ASSORTMENT

OF
ALL KINDS OF BRITISH

# PERFUMERY

FROM THE
FIRST HOUSES IN LONDON
AMONG WHICH ARE

## MRS. VINCENT'S
GENUINE

# GOWLAND'S LOTION

STANDS UNRIVALLED
FOR
CLEARING THE FACE AND SKIN,
From all Eruptions, Freckles, Extraordinary Redness, Effects of Surfeits Heat and Tumours, Scorbutic Impurities and , Dryness of the Skin, all Blotches and Pimples, from whatever cause arising. Hard Lumps of Knobs in the Skin,

the Greasy or Oily Appearance, livid and sickly Paleness, Thickness and Opacity, and for Clearing and improving the Complexion.

---

## DANCE LESSONS

EDWARD ANDERSON
Having lately arrived in Calcutta, respectfully begs leave to announce to the Ladies and Gentlemen of the Settlement, that he has taken a very commodious and airy House, No. 7, Circular Road (which he has named the Circular Hall,) where he will undertake to teach Young Ladies and Gentlemen the French Cotillion Dance, with a number of fashionable Figures; also the Waltz and Centruise Dance, Horn Pipe, &c. Two Lessons a week, either at home or a Monthly Ball, any Ladies and Gentlemen that wish to become Subscribers, will be pleased to address a Line to E.A.
The Subscription Book for the above undertaking remains in this Office, for the inspection of any Gentlemen or Ladies that wish to become Subscribers.

FROM THE CALCUTTA GAZETTE
Thursday. March 12, 1818. No. 1776.

---

## THEATRE

The Comic Opera of Rossina, was performed on Friday night to a less crowded audience than we expected. The scenery was beautiful; the parts were uniformly well sustained, and the performance, in general, gave great satisfaction.
Though the airs of this little piece, which are a compilation of Scotch and Irish, set by Shields, are well adapted, and the dialogue simple and natural; it seems too serious to be well calculated for the meridian of Calcutta.

The humour of Mr. O'Keefe's operas will ever render them more popular performances, in which conviction we are happy to hear that the AGREEABLE SURPRISE is in rehearsal, and will venture to say that from this exhibition the layers of music and of humour will receive ample satisfaction.

Previous to the Opera a very well-conceived prologue was delivered with much humour (as it is said) by the Author. – the point on which it principally turned, was the ridiculous effect gentlemen preparing behind the scenes for ladies characters, and an invitation to them to come forward; a measure however earnestly to be wished, not likely to be accomplished.
We have seen the Cologne Gazettes, which arrived yesterday, via. Bussora, as late as the 12$^{th}$ of June. The short time they were in our possession, however, has prevented us from making many extracts, but the following are the heads of the most essential Intelligence which they contain.

FROM THE CALCUTTA GAZETTE
Thursday. March 12, 1818. No. 1776.

---

Hicky's Bengal Gazette; or Calcutta General Advertiser.
Saturday April 1$^{st}$ to Saturday April 8$^{th}$, 1780. Page 4.

**SLAVES**

ELOPED.
From his Masters service about two months ago, and is supposed to have gone up the Country in the Service of some officer, a Little Slave Boy about twelve years old, can speak, read, and write English very well. Any Gentleman discovering such a person amongst his servants, and will give intelligence to the Printer it shall be thankfully received, by the Gentleman who has lost the boy.
Calcutta April 1, 1780.

Selections from the early newspaper print in colonial Calcutta.

## FIRE IN DANCING GIRLS HOUSES

Hicky's Bengal Gazette; or Calcutta General Advertiser.
April 22$^{nd}$, to april 29$^{th}$. 1780. no. XIV. Page 2.

CALCUTTA.
On Friday, 21$^{st}$, about five o' clock in the Afternoon a very great fire broke out in the Suba-bazaar at the bob Garden. The noted place of residence of the black Ladies of pleasure, one of whom was much burned, and now lays dangerously ill without hopes of recovery. She is the mother of Santhee Ram the famous Dancing Girl. It seems that several of our English Seamen was on a visit there to some of the sooty Beauties, when the fire begun which proved a very fortunate circumstance for some of their Ladies, as the Jacks not only saved their Lives by carrying them off but also returned to the houses and in the midst of the flames entered brought out the Chests that contained their Clothes, money and joys which they very generously returned them, and for which the Ladies has promised to reward the Jacks, with an Entertainment of Dancing, and Singing, a good Supper, plenty of Grogg and a nights Lodging of gratis, as soon as they can get fresh Houses built.

## NAUTCH GIRL

Hicky's Bengal Gazette; or Calcutta General Advertiser.
August the 18$^{th}$ to August 25$^{th}$, 1781. page 2.

AN ENTERTAINMENT.
On Monday Night, Rajah Nabobkissen gave a Nautch and Magnificent Entertainment to several persons of distinction in commemoration of Miss Wrangham's birthday. – As the Laoics

arrived, they were conducted by the Rajah through a grand suite of apartments into the Zenana. – where they were amused until the singing began – which was so mellifluous as to give every face a smile of approbation. – The surprising agility of one of the Male Dancers occasioned loud acclamations of applause.

---

## SUBSCRIPTION CONCERT AND A MUSICAL
# PROPOSALS FOR A
### FOR A
## SUBSCRIPTION CONCERT.

------------------

**MR. TRINKS,** who has on various occasions, been honoured with the patronage of the Ladies and Gentlemen of this Settlement, begs leave to submit to their consideration the following PROPOSALS for a CONCERT, which he means soon to exhibit, should his Plan meet with approbation and support.

FIRST. The best Band of Musicians shall be provided for the Concert, which will be held at the Old Court House.

SECOND. There will be Twelve Concerts in the year; the FIRST on TUESDAY the 4$^{th}$ of March next; to be continued every fortnight, whilst the weather will admit, but only once a month when the warm season commences.

THIRD.. The Subscription to be 150 Sicca Rupees.

FOURTH. The Tickets of Subscribers to be transferrable, and without which no Non-Subscriber can be admitted.

MR. TRINKS assures those Ladies and Gentlemen who may honour him with their patronage, that every endeavor, on his part, shall be exerted to merit their approbation, which he presumes to expect, as several Ladies, distinguished for their musical talents, have already given him the flattering hopes of their assistance, both in vocal and instrumental music – a circumstance that cannot fail to render the Concert, in general, a most agreeable entertainment.

…

FROM THE CALCUTTA GAZETTE, February 21, 1788.

---

## MUSICAL BANDS
## H.W. NEIDMAN

No. 159. NEW BOW-BAZAR.

*Late Band Master of H.M. 59th Regiment.*

Begs leave to inform the Ladies and Gentlemen of the Settlement, that he intends supplying them with a Band of Musicians, forming a complete Military Band, on the shortest notice, and on the most moderate terms. Mr. N. entertains not the least doubt of his giving entire satisfaction to those who may favour him with their orders. Mr. N. also gives Instructions on the following instruments:

VIOLIN, VIOLONCELLO, and TENOR, FLUTE.

And also undertakes to arrange Music for the different Instruments.

Likewise Tunes and Repairs Piano Forte.


From The CALCUTTA GAZETTE

Thursday, June 18, 1818.

## ADVERTISEMENTS.

## FOR SALE,

### AT THE

# French Warehouse,

### No. 9. DAGRE'S LANE,

*Near the Treasury.*

Jewellery; Musical Gold Snuff Boxes and Watches; Ladies' and Gentlemen's gold Watches; Morning Ornaments; black and white Net Dresses, worked in floss Silk; black and white Lace Gowns and Veils; Lyon's Silk Stuff; Artificial Flowers; Ladies and Gentlemen's Gloves; Ladies Shoes; Perfumery; Pier Glasses, some measuring 77 by 45 inches; most beautiful French Porcelain.

Also the undermentioned WINES and LIQUORS, warranted genuine, and equal to any heretofore imported:

Pink and while Champagne,
Claret Haut Brion,
Pichon Langueville,
Vin de Graves, St. Brys of the Year,     1805
Haut Barsac,                1805
Old Muscat de Frontignan,          do.
Old Cogniac Brandy.
Aniseed Liqueur of Marie Brizard.
White Wine and
Tarragon Vinegar.

N.B. The above articles are sold at moderate prices.

Selections from the early newspaper print in colonial Calcutta.

*All orders addressed to Mr. JOHN BETTS, No. 9. Dacre's Lane, will be punctually attended to.*

From The <u>CALCUTTA GAZETTE</u>. Thursday. June 18$^{th}$, 1818.

**THEATRE.**

# SUPPLEMENT

## TO THE

# CALCUTTA GAZETTE

THURSDAY. January, 17, 1788.

THEATRE.

THE FIRST FLOOR, on Tuesday evening went off somewhat paradoxically. The principal parts were certainly played well. *Young* and *Old Whimsey, Mrs. Pattipan, Nancy Tarilet,* and *Furnish* spoke and acted with spirit and humour. Yet the whole performance gave little satisfaction.

THE FLITCH OF BACON, had more success; many of the airs in it received great applause, and particularly a lively one sung by *Major Bembo,* whose comic attitudes, dress and manner repeatedly excited bursts of laughter, and afforded general entertainment.

The acting Manager of the Theatre, who has ever shown the greatest attention to promote entertainment, will, we trust, excuse the hint of a correspondent, that as one of the principal musical Gentlemen of the Settlement is soon about to take his departure from this country, the *Poor Soldier,* who was so universal a favourite, may not be forgotten, while he can be once more introduced to such advantage.

We understand that the Tragedy of King Richard the Third is in rehearsal, and will be performed soon.

---

## LECTURE ON THE SCIENCES.

# Experimental Philosophy.

At the EXCHANGE COFFEE ROOM, the THIRD LECTURE will be Read THIS EVENING, at half past Seven o' Clock.
It will commence with the Experiments of the Leyden Phial, and Electrical Battery.
Some interesting Experiments made in England will be imitated, and applied to the construction of Conductors of Lighting.
The History of Electricity will be continued down to the present time.
Some of the most striking and sublime operations of Nature will be referred to Electrical Phenomena, and explained on Electrical Principles.
And this part of the Course will determine with those beautiful Experiments, which are thought to exhibit, in a sensible manner, the passage of the Electrical Fluid, according to the Franklinian Theory.
TICKETS for the Course at FIVE GOLD MOHURS, are delivered at the GENERAL, BENGAL, AND INDOSTAN BANKS.
AND, TICKETS for each Reading at TWELVE SICCA RUPEES, at the EXCHANGE.

From The <u>CALCUTTA GAZETTE</u>. Oct. 16$^{th}$. 1788. Vol. X.

Selections from the early newspaper print in colonial Calcutta.

---

## ADVERTISEMENTS FROM

From The <u>CALCUTTA GAZETTE</u>. August, 23$^{rd}$, 1787.

Commission Ware-House,

LEE, SANDERS, & KENNEDY.

HAVE RECEIVED FOR SALE,

A STOCK of London particular and London market Madeira Wines, with a quantity of old hock, and coniac brandy, from a house lately dissolved partnership, and now explore them for SALE at reasonable rates. They will be warranted as good as any in Calcutta.

*For* S A L E

*At No. 139, in the Rada Bazar,*

LADY'S AND GENTLEMEN'S ROYAL

SCOTCH VELVET BONNETS,

With or without FEATHERS.

**WANTED A FEMALE TEACHER.**

O R P H A N  S O C I E T Y.

WANTED a discreet middle aged EUROPEAN WOMAN, who can teach reading and plain work, to assist in the care of Female Children under the direction of the Governess of the daughters of Officers at the Orphan House. Any one who thinks herself qualified, must apply to Mr. Henchman, the Deputy Governor, or to Mr. Ackland, the Secretary.

By order of the Deputy Governor,
and Managers,
HENRY ACKLAND, *Sec.*

## CARPENTERS.

*Messrs.* DEXTER & LANE,

Most respectfully beg leave to inform the Gentlemen of the settlement, and the public in general, that they have entered into partnership, to carry on the trade of SMITHS and CARPENTERS in all their branches. Mr. Lane also begs leave to inform, the Gentlemen of the settlement, and the public in general, that as he has been an assistant to Messrs. Candler and Mr. Nicoll for these three years past, he hopes to give the utmost satisfaction to those Gentlemen who may please to honour him with their commands; all sorts of Carpenters work, Carriages made and repaired on very reasonable terms.

## A RAFFLE

THE SCHEME and PROPOSAL for Raffling the elegant and high finished FINGER and BARRELL ORGAN, imported on the BRITTANIA, CAPT. CUMMING, at 250 S. Rs. per chance, is now opened for Subscribers at the house of POPE, FAIRLIE, and CAMPBELL, and will take place as soon as twenty four chances are filled up.

N.B. The Organ is complete, and in the best order.

## SERVICES OF AN UNDERTAKER.

*By* JAMES PALMER, *Undertaker,*
*Rada Bazar.*
Tombs and Monuments erected.
Epitaphs and Inscriptions cut.
*On the most reasonable terms.*

Selections from the early newspaper print in colonial Calcutta.

*A large assortment of*
Black and White Marble Slabs.

---

**NATIVE SERVANTS.**

# Hints on Native Rougery

To the Editor of the Calcutta Journal.

SIR,
A worthy English Gentlemen, who I know wishes me well, and secretly admits of my Visits in a most kind manner interrogated me at my last interview much in this way" "But what is the reason that the Natives are all considered rogues? Everyone of my acquaintance say, they are not be depended upon." A very *wholesome* assertion truly, Mr. Editor; and as I then, I hope, satisfied the Querist with the answer I made, I trust it will not be deemed irrelevant if I subjoin it in defense of my Countrymen, and this the more particularly, seeing from the nature of the assertion that it is generally believed to be founded in truth.

I fired a random shot, and for *illustration alone* fixed upon the Custom House. Let any one, says I, look at the Native Establishment employed there, the salaries they receive, the respectability of the situation, expenses incident thereto, and can he wonder that dishonesty should be resorted to, to obtain what the most faithful discharge of official duty will not obtain. Take an instance. The Head Native Officer. What is his salary? Fifty rupees per month. Can a man in that (in the eyes of his countrymen) high and respectable situation subsist upon that trifle and keep a conveyance in the bargain? Certainly not, if he has not other resources. It is very clear that when a native succeeds to one of these appointments, he is very closely watched, has not the power, even if he had the inclination to receive bribes, knows that his salary will not meet his expenses, and being fond of adulation and respect, continues holding the appointment till a press of expenses obliges him at length to make one effort to extricate himself, and that terminates most probably in his loss of office.

...

         I am, Sir, your obedient sevant,
         SIBNARAIN CHUNDER.

*Jorasanko*
*July 29, 1819.*

FROM THE CALCUTTA JOURNAL. August 11, 1819.

---

**BATHS AND FLOORING.**

Marble Baths, Flooring
for Halls, &c.

The practice now universally adopted among the genteel families of this settlement, of having BATHS in their houses, lined, or only floored with MARBLE SLABS, likewise Halls, and other Apartments induces JAMES PALMER, (No.39, Rada Bazar), to acquaint the LADIES and GENTLEMEN of the settlement, that he has lately purchased a large Assortment of MARBLE SLABS, for the above mentioned purposes. He erects MARBLE BATHS, and lays MARBLE FLOORS in Halls and other Apartments, on the most reasonable Terms.

From <u>The Calcutta Gazette</u>, Thursday April 17, 1788, Vol.9, No.216, p.3, column.4.

---

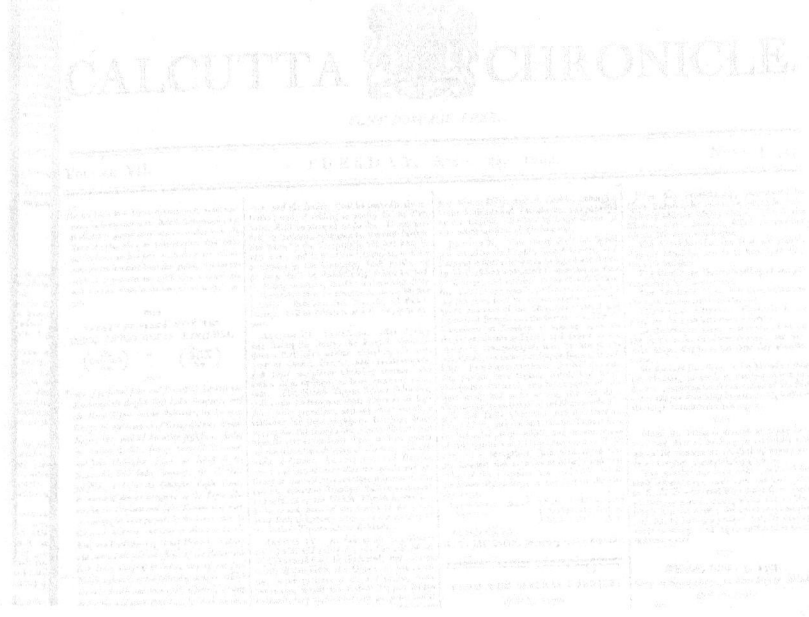

## 5 POETRY, PRINT AND THE PRESS

No eighteenth-century book in England emerged from the printer without "pages of advertisements, printed or pasted onto the back," thus allowing for print to promote print.[15] Consumer fetishism was not limited to the use of material things, and a similar desire is evident in how printed texts were published and consumed in Calcutta. The advertisements in the newspapers allow us to gauge the nature of the communication network between author, reader, printer, and publisher that was evident in Calcutta.

The newspapers and books that were printed in Calcutta, based on subscription readership, ensured the printers a sense of economic viability. This model of subscription publication was a system in use in eighteenth century England. Till the seventeenth century, there had been censorship in England, allowing the government control and surveillance of the kinds of books that were printed, and the number of books that could be printed. With the lapse of the Licensing Act in 1695, a free sphere of print culture evolved, without systematic government intervention. John Brewer describes the emergence of this realm of eighteenth century printers and publishers.[16] In 1689,

---

[15] Barbara Benedict, Readers, Writers, Reviewers and the Professionalization of Literature (Cambridge: Cambridge University Press, 2006), p. 7.

[16] John Brewer, "Authors, Publishers and the Making of Literary Culture," in The

the world of printing was limited to a few sections of London in St. Paul's Churchyard and Paternoster Row, dominated by a powerful trade guild, and was a community where everyone knew everybody else. But a hundred years later, the publishing industry had grown and in 1785, John Pendred wrote the first guide to English publishing which covered the provinces: *The London and Country Printers, Booksellers and Stationers Vade Mecum.* What "had begun as a London trade had become a national business."[17] The rise of the periodical press made it possible for the professional writer to emerge, and have a career based solely on writing. Commercial publishing meant the bookseller had the upper hand in determining what kinds of books were to be printed, displayed, and were sales-worthy. Subscription made it possible for the inevitable commercial viability in the market place, and the independence of the author as it implied a certain amount of sales, which covered production and distribution costs. The eighteenth century saw subscription publication emerge, bringing together the interests of the author, patron and bookseller. The subscriber had become the patron—which in the earlier centuries was the role played by the Court or wealthy individuals. This model was followed by the printers and writers in Calcutta, and ensured some degree of economic independence for emergent writers.

With the emergence of subscription readership the relationship between the author, reader and printer changed. Newspapers played a role in disseminating news about new publishing ventures, becoming a medium though which new printing enterprises were advertised and therefore, it was through print that a desire for more print was created and sustained.

---

Book History Reader, ed. David Finkelstein and Alistair McCleery (London and New York: Routledge, 2002).

[17] Ibid., p. 244.

## ADVERTISEMENTS.

<u>CALCUTTA GAZETTE</u>
TUESDAY, SEPTEMBER 29, 1818. NO. 1805.

ADVERTISEMENTS
TO THE SUBSCRIBERS
TO THE
CALCUTTA GAZETTE
AND
MORNING POST
NEWSPAPERS
AND
TO THE PUBLIC AT LARGE.

The proprietors of the Calcutta Gazette and of the Morning Post being about to close these Papers, return thanks to their respective Subscribers for the patronage which they have shown them, and respectfully solicit both from them and from the Public in general, the continuation of that patronage in favor of a New Paper to be substituted in their stead, the first Number of which will be published on Friday, the 24$^{th}$ of October, and the plan and arrangement of which are fully detailed in the following Prospectus:
PROSPECTUS OF A NEW PAPER,
TO BE ENTITILED
THE CALCUTTA JOURNAL
OR,
POLITICAL, COMMERCIAL, AND LITERARY GAZETTE.

"A forward retention of custom is as turbulent a thing as innovation, and they that reverence too much old times are but a scorn to the new." – Bacon.

The state of the Press has been a subject of surprise, of disappointment, and of regret, to all strangers on their first arrival in India; and though the impression of its imperfections gradually loses its force after a long residence in the country, yet some of its ablest apologies and most zealous supporters acknowledge its reforms to be a desideratum.

Within the city of Calcutta alone, there are no less than nine Public Gazettes, each of them offering itself as the organ of public sentiment, each of them professing to have the earliest intelligence of great events, and each of them promising their portion of original disquisition. With the exception of two or three atmost, these Journals are found however to have no sentiment, either of the public or of their own, on the leading features of the times, no earlier intelligence of great events than that which they have copied from their 'brother editor' of the preceding day, and no more of original disquisition than has been evolved, from the Prints of Europe to those of India, and then, in sevenfold repetition, from one to the other, till the weekly round has been completed.

Yet amid this absence of novelty, Supplement follows after Supplement, in such a multiplied succession as to induce a stranger to suppose that the influx of new information was more rapid than the Press could keep pace with. Custom has established and bad taste retains the practice of filling up a certain number of closely printed columns, the subjects of which in the dearth of general news, are indiscriminately drawn from old files of English Papers already more than exhausted and dilated on to an extreme of tedious prolixity.

# LIBRARY

Hicky's <u>Bengal Gazette; or Calcutta General Advertiser</u>.

LIBRARY.
July 14th to July 21st. 1781. No. XXVI.
Page 2.
Public Library.
John Andrews Respectfully begs leave to Inform the Ladies and Gentlemen of the Settlement, that the Circulating Library kept hitherto in the Old Fort, is removed to a Cool and Commodious House formerly belonging to Doctor Hamilton behind the Riding School, and Between the Houses of George Livius Esqr. And Mr. Schultz Jeweller.

---

# PUBLICATIONS.

<u>The Calcutta Gazette,</u>

Thursday, February 28, 1788, Vol.8, No.209, p.2, column 3.

On Friday the 7th of next Month
WILL BE PUBLISHED,
THE
MEMOIRS
OF
Khojeh Abdulkurreem,
A Cashmerian of Distinction;
Who accompanied NADIR SHAH, on his return from HINDOSTAN to PERSIA; from whence he traveled to BAGDAD, DAMASCUS, and ALEPPO; and after visiting MEDINA and

MECCA, embarked on a ship at the port of JEDDEH, and sailed to Hooghly in Bengal.

INCLUDING
THE HISTORY OF HINDOSTAN
from A.D 1739 to 1749:
With an account of the EUROPEAN SETTLEMENTS in BENGAL, and on the Coast of Coromandel.

*Translated from the Original Persian,*
BY
FRANCIS GLADWIN, ESQ.
PRICE, ONE GOLD MOHUR.

---

## NEW PUBLICATION.

Just Published
A
NARRATIVE
OF THE
Transactions in Bengal,
During the SOOBAHDARIES of
AZEEM USSHAN, JAFFER KHAN, SHUJA KHAN, SIRAFRAZ KHAN, and ALYVIRDY KHAN.

*Translated from the Original Persian*
BY
FRANCIS GLADWIN, ESQ.
To be had at the LIBRARY,
(PRICE ONE GOLD MOHUR.)

Just Published

(Price Two GOLD MOHURS)

By *T. JONES*,
*At his Printing Office.*
No, 33, RADA BAZAR.

The whole of the PROCEEDINGS of the COURT MARTIAL and TRIAL
At CIVIL LAW, in the cause of THOMAS and BRISTOW.

From the decision in this cause, an appeal has been lodged; such Gentlemen as are desirous of being furnished with the reasons upon which it is grounded, are requested to signify their wishes to Mr. JONES.

## UNPUNCTUAL CIRCULATION.

### Madras Courier

THE EDITORS, with best respects to the Public, in proportion to the demand for THEIR PAPER, are sorry to receive from so many respectable authorities, complaints of its unpunctual circulation. They now beg to assure the Public, that they may in future depend on the most exact punctuality for the delivery of the COURIER, and the insertion of ESSAYS and ADVERTISMENTS in that Paper, by application to their present Agents Messrs. HAMILTON and ABERDEIN, Calcutta; or to Mr. JONES, at Messrs. CORBETT and BOYD'S Fort St. George.

*Fort St. George, April 5, 1788*

N.B. Such Gentlemen as wish to be supplied with
   The Madras Almanac and Civil List, -  S.Rs. 6
   Or List of the Army,                  -    - 10
   Or Military Regulations,              -      16

All just published, will please apply as above.

From <u>The Calcutta Gazette</u>, Thursday, May 1, 1788, Vol.9, No.218, p.3, column.3

---

**BOOKKEEPER.**

<u>The Calcutta Gazette</u>, Thursday, May 1, 1788, Vol.9, No.218, p.3, column.3

*WANTED*

AN EXPERINECED

BOOK-KEEPER.

Apply to the Printer.

---

**POETRY.**

*POET'S CORNER.*
*Addressed to Mrss.* F___T__M.

Tis not my Jenny's sparking eyes,
Her air, her early grace;
Her thrilling accents that I prize,
Or yet her blooming face__

Such charm as these, in others shine,
Whose beauty's all they boast;
As when that beauty does decline,
Their greater power is lost.___

As these that raise the maiden's fame,
That prompt desire and love;
And kindle in my breath a flame,
That time can ne'er remove.___

Calcutta Chronicle, August, 1787.

---

ADVERTISEMENT OF A GUJRATHI NEWSPAPER.

# SUPPLEMENT TO THE CALCUTTA CHORNICLE.

CALCUTTA – SATURDAY EVENING, MAY 8<sup>TH</sup>, 1832.

### 𝔅𝔬𝔪𝔟𝔞𝔭

We have to announce to our readers the establishment of a new Gujrathee News Paper called "Jami Jamsheed," which has been set on foot by a Parsee Gentleman, within the last few weeks. It is published weekly, on Mondays, and contains, for the most part, translations of Papers of this Presidency, and commercial intelligence, which cannot fair to make the paper acceptable to a mercantile community like that of Bombay. The extremely neat, and decidedly superior, of that of any the Goojrathee Papers hitherto published at this place – and advantage for which it is indebted to lithography, in which it is executed, and which is much better suited to the oriental character than typograohy.

In another part of this Paper, will be found an Advertisement acquainting the public that there is for sale a work both in English and Marathee, entitled "an Exposure of the Hindu Religion," by the Revd. Mr. Wilson, being a reply to Morephutt [sic] Dandekar's *Hindu Dharma Sthabana*. In the preface to Mr. Wilson's English book, a short account is given of the public discussion which took place last year between him and Morephutt, [sic]... We believe Morebhutt is the first instance of a Brahman coming forwards publicly to vindicate the Hindu Religion and entering the field of public discussion publishing a work in defence. – Bom. Dur.

---

**CIRCULATING LIBRARY.**

# CALCUTTA
## CIRCULATING LIBRARY

MESSRS. COCK, MAXWELL, and Co. conceiving that a CIRCULATING LIBRARY on the same plan with that at the Presidency, would be found a great convenience to gentlemen at a distance, who cannot procure Books otherwise than by purchase, and they having now so large a collection on hand as to enable them to divide the same, and yet retain a sufficient number for the use of Calcutta, they propose establishing a LIBRARY at BEHRAMPORE, and also to furnish a

Correspondent at DINAPORE and CAWNPORE with Books for circulation at those Stations and in their vicinity provided a sufficient number of Subscribers shall be found to defray the expenses. – And for the accommodation of the gentlemen in the medical line at the different Stations above mentioned, they will furnish a collection of the most approved ancient and modern authors on Medicine, Surgery, Anatomy, and Chymistry.

Should their plan meet with approbation, the Subscribers may be assured that no pains or expense will be spared to render it useful. – The Subscription to be the same as in Calcutta, viz. 8 Sicca Rupees per month.

Public notice will soon be given of the persons who will receive Subscription at the different Stations: in the mean time such gentlemen as may approve the plan, will be pleased to signify the same to Messrs. COCK, MAXWELL, and Co. in Calcutta.

FROM THE <u>CALCUTTA GAZETTE</u>; FEB 21$^{TH}$, 1788)

Selections from the early newspaper print in colonial Calcutta.

## ON FREEDOM OF THE PRESS.

# SUPPLEMENT TO THE CALCUTTA GAZETTE

### THURDAY, MAY 14, 1818.

### THE TIMES, NOVEMBER 21, 1817.

### LIBERTY OF THE PRESS.

Baron Pasquier, Keeper of the Seal, then mounted the Tribune and spoke as follows:

"Gentlemen, the project of the law, which we have the honour of presenting to you, ought to exite your attention in a more special manner, because it aims at accomplishing two objects, both equally important. The first is to preserve and secure the exercise of the liberty of the press, consecrated by the charter, by giving to the public authority, the means of separating its legitimate use from the abuse which may result from it; the second, to retain for the Government a protecting power, which you placed in its hands during the last session, and which the political situation of the country still requires, notwithstanding the ameriolation in its circumstances.

"The 8th article of the Constitutional Charter is couched in those words: - 'Frenchmen have a right to publish and to cause to be published, their opinions, in conformity, however, with the laws which must repress the abuse of this liberty.'

"Every reflecting mind has admitted, that the liberty of the press would not be complete, and that it could not be enjoyed with entire security, until a law, doubtless difficult to frame, but most indispensable, should provide for the prevention of all its abuses. …"

"It is not necessary, in this assembly, to develop the advantages of the press; you know them; as citizens, as deputies and friends of science, you consider that they are inherent in our rights, and ought to be regarded as one of the surest guarantees for the constitution of the State. … Uncurbed licentiousness would degenerate into confusion and oppression. Such impunity would leave society and citizens unprotected.

"If the writer, who publishes a dangerous work, and one that is contrary in the laws, were not responsible for what he did, the crimes of the press would be privileged; the legislators must use two weights and two measures. …
…
"The liberty of the press may be abused by publishing dangerous or injurious works. Reason and justice require that he who has done the mischief and committed the abuse, should be responsible for them. Thence arises the principle of the responsibility of the author.

---

**REPUBLICATION THROUGH SUBSCRIPTION.**

**From The Calcutta Gazette/ Thursday. June 18, 1818.**

# PROPOSALS

## FOR RE-PRINTING BY SUBSCRIPTION,

### (AN IMPROVED EDITION)

## N.G. DUFIEF'S

Selections from the early newspaper print in colonial Calcutta.

IN HER MODE OF TEACHING LANGUAGE TO MAN: OR A NEW AND INFALLIBLE METHOD OF,

# ACQUIRING A LANGUAGE
## IN THE SHORTEST TIME POSSIBLE

Deduced from the Analysis of the Human Mind, and consequently suited to every Capacity.

## ADAPTED TO THE FRENCH.

The work entitled "Nature Displayed &c.&c." by Monsieur N.G. Dufief of Philadelphia, stands in need of no recommendation to those who have had an opportunity by actual examination of its plans and contents, of themselves appreciating its merits. For the sake of others, it is proposed here to quote the sentiments of those critics who have noticed it, to insert a specimen of the work itself, and finally to state the remarkable circumstances which have led to the design of republishing it in this country.

It has passed through three editions in the United States…
…

In the year 1814, a member of the literary society in this city, who had seen M.Dufief's work, happening to mention it in terms of high praise, general interest and curiosity were excited, and the secretary was desired to spare no pains or expense in order to procure a copy for the society. Every enquiry was made in Calcutta: but in vain. Peace and renewal of intercourse taking place with the United States, two supercargoes of American Vessels that had arrived in this port, were requested on their return to their own country to send a few copies of the whole of M/Bufief's works. One of them who lately arrived in the river reported that not a copy was procurable in Boston. The accounts received from America state that all the editions have been exhausted, and that the author has no present intention of issuing a fresh one.

In 1816, Mr. King, supercargo of the American Ship Pallas, had the kindness to present a member of the society alluded to with the valuable gift of a copy of "Nature Displayed," 2d.edition. No sooner had he received it than his friends began to solicit the loan of it, and after they had seen it eagerly to impress him to republish. He was too long deterred by the certain heavy expense attending the undertaking and the doubt, whether, notwithstanding the indisputable merit of the work, a sufficiently expensive rent could be anticipated. ... These were the same day shown to the Secretary of the Calcutta School Book Society, who happened to be no stranger to the work, having in December last found a copy of the 3d. edition among the books of the Reverend Mr. May of Chinsurah, and subsequently drawn the attention of the Committee to it. All the members being equally penetrated with a sense of its value and importance, it has been unanimously resolved to commission the whole of the works of M. Dufief from America.

Selections from the early newspaper print in colonial Calcutta.

ESTABLISHING A LITERARY SOCIETY.

# THE CALCUTTA JOURNAL

OR,

## Political, Commercial, and Literary Gazette.

Sunday, July 11, 1819.

### Literary Society

In continuation of our endeavors to excite in the public mind, some interests in pursuits that have of late fallen into neglect; to rouse some of the latent sparks of genius, talent and the power of investigation, which must exist tho' they lie dormant and inactive; and to diffuse throughout the community of India some portion of that love of Information, respect of Science, and due estimation of Philosophical Research, which characterizes the land of our birth, and gives to Britain the proud pre-eminence that she enjoys over all the nations of the earth; we present to them in our columns of to-day a document which deserves their deepest attention.
…
We should have been happy to have closed this sketch with a notice of some similar Institution among us here in Calcutta. The reputation of the Asiatic Society, the transcendent abilities and refined taste of its Founder, the talents of its succeeding Presidents, and the mass of erudition and accurate research displayed in their valuable labours which are already before the world; render any eulogium on the excellence of this Establishment quite unnecessary. But their investigation are confined to Oriental

Literature, and are carried on slowly, with all the patient examination that such abstruse subjects requires, and always in the tranquility of retirement from the noise and bustle of active or fashionable life.

**POETRY.**

# FROM THE CALCUTTA GAZETTE, OR THE ORIENTAL ADVERTISER

THURSDAY, NOVEMBER 29$^{TH}$, 1787.

To The EDITOR of the CALCUTTA GAZETTE

SIR,
A MAN who has the least portion of leisure to bestow on the various publications of the day, will not hesitate to pronounce this to the Poetical Age. – No *Lady* or *Gentlemen* (we have no *men* and *women*) can now experience any of the accidents which attend our mortal Pilgrimage, such as the being married, ruined, cuckolded, imprisoned, or hanged; nor enjoy the rational pleasures of dancing, …coquetting, gambling, dressing etc. but the muses begin their song, and Apollo tunes his fiddle, - The immortal strains are suffered to reach us through the medium of the *fiery energy* of HAYLEY's majestic numbers, the soft *simplicity* and *unadorned* style of the gentle SEWARD, and the pretty warblings of the new-fledged WILLIAMS – Bristol sends forth her pipe makers and milk maids, and London trains her pigs to letters, that they also may become the vehicles of song. We are, in short, a nation of

Poets – A compensation sufficient to console us for the loss of Empire; and of character, both public and private. – At so favourable a juncture, when criticism is exploded as cruel, wit as rudeness, and learning as pedantry, when our taste is so purified that a CHARLOTTE SMITH dies unlamented, and her sonnets (worthless because they speak the mere language of nature) lie unread, permit me, Mr. Editor, to contribute my mite to the general stock of rhyme, scrawled over a dish of tea in a happy moment of vacuity. – Should it meet with a favourable reception, I shall from time to time indulge the pleasing propensity, in hopes that although I, may not obtain a seat at their tea-table, yet that I may arrive at the honour of holding up the tails, or carrying the pattern, of the muses od my Lords.
CARLISLE, PALMERTON, or MULGRAVE.

A MADRIGAL
FOR me my fair a Pudding made,
Where choicest tastes in union meet,
When smoking on the dresser laid,
Its steam gave sweetness to the sweet.

A whelp that to the kitchen stole,
To steal a bone and get a sop,
Beheld it from his lurking hole,
And out the ugly cur did pop.

No more he thought of skin or ferag,
Disdaining all his former prey;
Th' ungrateful spoiler left the bag,
But with the pudding ran away.

    I am, SIR,

Your Humble Servant,
P.P.


MR. EDITOR.
If you think the following lines, in reply to the Gentlemen who appeared in the Poet's Corner of your left, under the signature of ADMINISTRATOR, have any merit, pray insert them.   M.


O THOU lofty thoughts disclaim,
The beaten, vulgar track to fame,
Whose bold ambition can dispense
With wit, and laugh at common sense,
Whose fiery Peg – disdaining check,
Regardless of his rider's neck,
Thro' thick and thin explores his way
And kicks at all the critics say;
Thy bold Pindarics clearly prove,
Nonsense is eloquence in love.

But if your Nag, wou'd condescend,
To bait a bait a bit, and hear a friend.
Just for a private word or two,
'Twill neither injure him or you,
First, I advice, if e'er again,
The muse shou'd prompt your teeming brain,
And woe the while – if 'tis decrees,
That you must write, and we must read,
Before your Genius bursts away,
Reflect on what you're going to say,
For you've a pretty knack at metre,
And sure no lark, e'er warb'led sweeter.

Yet rhime without consideration,
But badly pleads for *Admiration*,
Stuck as we are at the confusion
That flounders thro' each bold allusion;
For what the Devil has warriors toils
To do with any body's smiles?
When fury wild destruction scatters,
Are wounds and death such laughing matters?

Or can your Esculapians say?
Their skill contributes to display,
One pleasant look or smiling grace
When anguish grinds the patients face,
Tho' "Vers'd in nature's good and vile"
Their Sapient brows, disdains a smile.

The sons of Eloquence 'tis true,
May make us smile and so can you,
Let nonsense take what form it will,
In prose or verse, 'tis nonsense still,
And may obtain, from sheer vexation
A smile – but not approbation.

Painters the human face may dress,
And Poets labor to express,
The smile you talk of, but in vain,
The Painter's art, or Poet's brain –
Both must the weak attempt deplore,
And fall, as you have fall'n before.

And when you start again for fame,
In pity spare your fair one's name,

If you reflect upon the matter,
You'll find such praise is downright satire,
You'll ne'er the wish'd-for bliss obtain
While folly tags each tedious strain,
Tho' you in sweet persuasive style
Plead for "a youth devoid of guile,"
So sweetly flows you're plaintive moan,
It makes e'en the Poet's Corner groan,
But if the she scorns the suppliant smile,
And still continues to refuse,
I'd write no more, and so perplex her
Or hang or drown myself to vex her.

## ON LETTERS.

FROM THE CALCUTTA JOURNAL. AUGUST 11, 1819.

To the Editor of the Calcutta Journal,

Heavy complaints have been made of the careless manner in which letters are sent out from England, and some fillips have been bestowed upon the Post Office at this Presidency. It seems to me that the Public has a just additional ground of complaint in the great delay which the Company's Ships, having Letter Packets on board, are allowed to make in proceeding from Other Presidencies to the port of their ultimate destination. We know that the Rose arrived at Madras some time ago, and the Minerva anchored off that Settlement a considerable number of days before the Rose. Passengers who came from England in the Minerva, and who left that ship in Madras, reached Calcutta about a fortnight since. But where are our Commercial Advices; where our notices of Bills *accepted* and *protested*; where our anxiously expected letters from tenderly loved relatives, giving interesting accounts of the first abecedical [sic] accounts of our far distant children. This, Mr. Editor, is an evil under the sun which requires correction.

I remain, Sir,<br>
Your humble servant,<br>
A FATHER AND SENIOR MERCHANT.

*Old Post Office street*
*August 10, 1819.*

# 6 APPENDIX

# APPENDIX.

**Seventeenth century newsbooks.**

The history of newspapers in England is a recent one, for printed news emerged in England only towards the early eighteenth century; Ian Atherton writes that till then, manuscripts were the most important form of written news as it was more accurate, less censored, and regarded as more authoritative.[18] For the historians also "it usually makes a better form of historical evidence."[19] Most news of the seventeenth century spread through word of mouth and this time period also saw an increase in political news. All forms of written news – newsbook and newspaper, pamphlets, newsletters, sermons, plays, and ballads -- depended heavily on oral news, and the last four were at the "interface between the oral and the written."[20] Interestingly enough, most of the news that was

---

[18] Ian Atherton, "The Itch grown a disease: Manuscript Transmission of News in the Seventeenth Century." in <u>News, Newspaper and Society in Early Modern Britain</u>, ed. Joan Raymond (London: Frank Cass, 1999), p. 39-65; p. 40.

[19] Ibid., p. 40.

[20] Ibid., p. 39.

conveyed was foreign; as in the 1620s and 1630s it was illegal to print domestic news in England, making censorship of manuscript news lighter, it was inevitable that the handwritten newsletters would be popular.[21] The writing of newsletters was an accomplishment that the gentry were expected to possess.[22] A central literary issue in the seventeenth century was the relationship between fact and fiction, and the development of the English newspaper has to be seen within this context where there was an "epistemological barrier between knowledge and opinion."[23]

There were social factors that determined who had access to what kinds of news: printed news – a product of the English Revolution -- was for the masses while newsletters, were for the elite.[24] Moreover, newsbook circulation was broad and socially diverse, "crossing barriers of social distinction where newsletters had not [done so]"; newbooks were in the public sphere, whereas newsletters belonged to the more private world of correspondence. Mass production and sale by booksellers or hawkers of printed news did away with the more direct relationship between the writer and reader of the newsletters. Often, printed newsbooks were mouthpieces of the ruling political parties[25] and by the 1680s, the "genres of the newsletters [impartial manuscript news] and the newspaper had virtually converged."[26] The circulation of news was

---

[21] Ibid., p. 42.

[22] Ibid., p. 44.

[23] Ibid., p. 48.

[24] Ibid., p. 52.

[25] Ibid., p. 53.

[26] Ibid., p. 55.

also seen as an act that, through its democratizing effect, spread to the vulgar, and state matters once accessible only to a select readership based on education and birth, had become a part of the common discourse of the masses.[27]

## Newspapers and British Imperial Identity

The newspaper print culture in eighteenth century England was able to bind the people within the frame of imperial citizenry, and even those in the provinces identified with the political processes of the state, nation and empire. Most newspapers carried news of war, trade and imperial expansion, shaping the readers notions of the nation and the empire, and British national identity rested on incorporating the colonies within the national imaginary.[28] The print-induced English sub-public was replete with images of the colonies where the British Empire spread across continents. For example, a review of Nathaniel Halhed's *Grammar of the Bengal Language* in the *English Review* in 1783 makes an easy equation between the study of Indian languages and their use in maintaining the British empire in India; "… we shall confine our observations to strictures on the history and usefulness of a language of very high antiquity, spoken by millions of industrious British subjects."[29] For Halhed, the British Empire embraced the newly formed native subjects into becoming "industrious British subjects."

---

[27] Ibid. p. 56.

[28] Ian Atherton, It was a seventeenth century commonplace that history could teach useful lessons. … Gentlemen were adviced to study history for delight and profit. Civil or political history was considered to be none other than an accurate report of past and present facts and events. Reading contemporary history – the news – could, therefore, be as profitable as reading ancient history." 45-46.

[29] "Review of Halhed's Grammar of the Bengal Language," The English Review, or, An Abstract of English and Foreign Literature 1(1783): 5-14.

Selections from the early newspaper print in colonial Calcutta.

# ABOUT
# FACSIMILE: A CENTER FOR EARLY PRINT AND SOCIETY

Facsimile is an independent research center that works on early print and society in colonial India. It is relevant to remember that print started in Calcutta, India, with the emergence of the East India company in the last two decades of the 18th century.
For more information, please visit us at:
www.colonialprint.wordpress.com

Also, visit www.earlycolonialprint.org to learn more about the emergence of early print in colonial Bengal, India.

www.ingramcontent.com/pod-product-compliance
Lightning Source LLC
Chambersburg PA
CBHW060722030426
42337CB00017B/2963